TILBURY HOUSE PUBLISHERS

12 Starr Street, Thomaston, Maine 04861

800-582-1899 • www.tilburyhouse.com

Hardcover ISBN 978-088448-561-2

First hardcover printing May 2018

15 16 17 18 19 20 XXX 10 9 8 7 6 5 4 3 2 1

Library of Congress Control Number: 2018936802

Cover and interior designed by Frame25 Productions

Printed in China

To K & J, who light up my life.

—NR

For Silas, with love. Keep discovering the world.

—CS

# The World Never Sleeps

Natalie Rompella

Illustrated by Carol Schwartz

TILBURY HOUSE PUBLISHERS, THOMASTON, MAINE

*Midnight.* *Stars speckle the darkness with bits of light.*

A cockroach skitters across the kitchen floor to snatch a forgotten breadcrumb.

In the backyard, a spider weaves an intricate design on the fence. Winged insects dance and flicker in the porch light.

Day and night, small creatures are busy working, eating, hunting, hiding.

*Deep in the night.* Moonlight fills in open spaces, mirroring the sun's light.

A female house centipede has been living behind the damp basement sink, but she isn't the only one hiding in the basement. Young house centipedes are also there. Now, in the night, they are hunting for a tasty morsel: a spiderling, a cockroach, a silverfish, or some fly larvae.

*Just before dawn.* Moonflowers soak in the last of the moonlight, while peonies and poppies sleep on, their soft petals tucked inside.

*Chirp, chirp.* A cricket calls from a wondrous spot that makes his sounds resonate. But when the sun rises, he will grow quiet and fall into slumber in his temporary home.

*Sunrise.* The sun peeks through tree branches, illuminating leaves and waking birds.

The spider tidies up after feeding on a moth it captured during the night. Before turning in for the day, the spider carefully gathers and eats its web.

*Early morning.* Beads of dew dazzle the grass, stems, and leaves, but then mysteriously disappear into the air.

A tiny egg hatches beneath the surface of a pond. The life of a dragonfly begins. Breathing through its gills, the nymph and its newly hatched siblings make their way through the pond, searching for food. The dragonfly nymph passes tadpoles. Once it has molted and gotten bigger, it will be ready to catch and eat one. Right now, it will settle for tiny water fleas.

*Midmorning.* Sunflowers stretch toward the day-star. Other flowers open.

A creature that was once a caterpillar is ready to emerge as something else. After hanging from a tree branch and blowing gently with the wind, it has completed its change. The chrysalis thins and splits open, revealing folded art. The new life inside pushes free.

Now a butterfly, the creature works a potion from its body to its wings. At last it can flutter. It can flash its wings. It can fly.

**Noon.** *The sun, suspended high in the sky, erases shadows and dries the soil.*

A loveliness of ladybugs is enjoying lunch—little aphids that pepper a crop of soybeans. But the feast might end early. A barn swallow flies overhead, also interested in eating. Before it grabs a ladybug, it notices the creature's polka dots and flies away without snacking.

**Midafternoon.** *The petals of a hibiscus flower crinkle and shrivel, thirsty from the heat of the day.*

A forager honey bee has been busy since morning gathering sweet nectar. Now she rests a moment before flying home, where she will pass her nectar to house bees. In the hive, they will change the liquid into thick honey.

*Late afternoon.* The sky pushes away clouds and mimics the color of the sea.

*Wriggle, wriggle.* An earthworm burrows through the cool soil. The day is too hot and dry to be above ground. The worm squirms deeper and deeper. A rotted apple has worked its way down to the world beneath the ground. The worm takes small bits, slowly turning the apple back into earth.

*Early evening.* Like skyscrapers, shadows become lanky, stretching farther and farther across the ground as the sun drifts lower in the sky.

*"Shoo!"* A fly zooms out of the house where it has been trapped all day. As it tries to warm itself in the lowering sun, it feels a breeze—a predator is zeroing in. The fly bolts out of a dragonfly's reach and lands on a melon flower. What perfect luck.

*Sunset.* Strokes of pink stain the sky. A slight breeze cools the air.

After two summers in the water, a mayfly emerges onto land. Wings at last! But there isn't much time. She passes other insects snacking on leaves, berries, and even a fallen ice cream cone, but the mayfly doesn't eat. Food doesn't matter now. She is searching for a mate.

The twilight gets darker. There is so little time. At last she finds a cloud of male mayflies. Quickly she flies back to the water, drops her eggs, and quietly dies.

**Nightfall.** *Stars begin to show their faces: one, two, three—then thousands.*

A male lightning bug blinks once
and waits for a female lightning
bug to respond. He blinks again.
She winks back.

*It is midnight again.*

**The cockroach comes back
out of hiding to discover new treasures. The
spider spins a fresh design on the fence to capture another
meal. Small, winged creatures flitter and bask in the nearby
porch light.  Night and day, day and night, wings flutter,
insects nibble, eggs hatch. The world never sleeps.**

# House Centipedes

Although centipedes are not insects, they are fellow arthropods. As with insects, hard exo-skeletons support and protect their soft bodies.

Centipedes found in homes are usually house centipedes. Most in the United States are thought to be non-native animals introduced from Europe. They can be found outdoors but are most often seen in moist, cool basements, bathtubs, showers, and sinks.

Because these creatures feed on silverfish, bed bugs, and cock-roaches, they help control house pests.

First-stage larvae have only four pairs of legs, but each time they molt, they gain one or two more pairs of legs and segments. Adults have fifteen pairs of legs, each attached to a different segment. Seven dorsal plates overlie the seg-ments. The plates stabilize a centipede's body and allow it to dart about to catch prey and escape predators.

# Crickets

Most species of crickets are nocturnal. When morning comes, they are ready to rest. Crickets are related to grasshoppers and katydids, which also make chirping sounds. A male cricket rubs his wings together to chirp, and the colder it is, the slower he chirps. With some prac-tice, you can use a snowy tree cricket's chirps to estimate the outside temperature. Crickets do not go through a complete metamorphosis as other insects (such as moths and butterflies) do. Instead, their nymph stage looks like a smaller version of the adult it grows into. Other insects with an incomplete metamorphosis include praying mantises, cockroaches, and stink bugs.

# Orb Weaving Spiders

Spiders—like ticks, scorpions, and mites—have eight legs and are called arachnids. Though not insects, they too are arthropods.

Some spiders, such as orb weavers, build webs to trap insects. The spider starts with a single very thin thread, releasing it into the air. When a breeze catches the loose end of the thread and blows it against a surface, it attaches there. The spider then crosses the gap, adding a strong silk line. The web is built below this bridge thread.

As the web is created, the spider uses sticky silk for some lines, perfect for trapping creatures; strong, non-sticky threads are used as the frame by the spider. It can also use these lines to reach its prey without getting stuck in its own web. When the spider is ready to make a new web, it can reel in the old one, consume it, and reuse the silk proteins.

# Dragonflies

There is a reason why adult dragonflies are found near the water: Dragonflies begin their lives underwater in streams and pools, and females return there to lay their eggs. The eggs often hatch a week later, but the incubation time and the length of time the nymphs remain in the water depend on the species, the weather, the water temperature, and how much food the nymphs can find.

Nymphs eat many water creatures: seed shrimp, copepods, daphnia (water fleas), bloodworms, small fish, tadpoles, and even each other. Like other arthropods, they must molt to grow, breaking through their old exoskeleton and hardening a new one. The time between molts is called an *instar*.

# Butterflies

Although butterflies and moths belong to the same order of insects, called Lepidoptera, there are differences. One is how each transforms from a caterpillar to their adult stage. While most moth caterpillars wrap themselves in something such as a leaf, silk, or both, creating a cocoon, butterfly caterpillars use only their bodies as their protective case, called a chrysalis. As butterflies emerge, they must pump their wings with a clear blood called hemolymph.

# Ladybugs

A large gathering of ladybugs is called a "loveliness." Ladybugs, also called ladybird beetles, are helpful insects. They eat small pests such as aphids, which feed on crops and garden plants. Some farmers and gardeners use ladybugs as a natural pesticide. Ladybugs also have warning colorations to keep them from being eaten. Their patterns and colors signal to predators that they are bad tasting and poisonous.

# Honey Bees

Like ants, honey bees live in colonies. There are three kinds of honey bees—the queen, drones, and worker bees—each with a very important job. The worker bees, which are always female, do just what their name says. The older worker bees, called forager bees, sip nectar from flowers, add enzymes from their mouths to start converting the nectar to honey, and store it in their bodies in an organ called a honey stomach. When the foragers return to the hive, they give the liquid to house worker bees, who continue converting it into honey. The unripe honey is placed in honeycomb cells, and worker bees wave their wings to evaporate water from the honey, making it thicker. Cells are sealed when they are full of this ripe honey. When the honeycomb is filled with sealed cells, beekeepers harvest the honey.

Each colony has a queen bee. She is the only female that lays eggs. The worker bees care for the queen by feeding her and tending to her eggs and larvae. Drone bees are always male. Their job is to mate with a queen from another colony so she can produce new workers and queens.

## Earthworms

Earthworms are scavengers and decomposers. They are important to the environment because they eat plant and animal matter that we no longer need. In nature, they consume dead leaves and rotting wood, breaking them down into soil. Their tunnels create holes in the soil, which help with aeration. They are also added to compost bins because they eat leftover foods such as fruits and vegetables and turn them into a nutrient-rich soil.

## Flies

Flies are often considered pests, but they are important to our world in multiple ways. Many fly larvae, called maggots, are scavengers and eat dead plants and animals. Like bees and butterflies, flies are pollinators, helping to create fruit, seeds, and new flowers. They are also food for other insects and other animals.

Flies know when a creature or a fly swatter is coming their way because they feel a change in the air and have superb eyesight! Flies leave a surface by flying upward, similar to how a helicopter lifts off the ground, rather than flying off to one side. Fly swatters work because they come toward the fly when it tries to escape. The holes in the swatter help to surprise the fly because they don't create as much resistance as a newspaper or a hand does.

# Mayflies

Mayflies spend most of their lives in the water—some as much as four years. When they finally emerge, they quickly molt, becoming pre-adults and having wings. Then they fly away from the water, and, unlike other winged insects, molt a second time.

Mayflies live in water that is not heavily polluted. Because of this, they are considered bioindicators—they help scientists know whether a water source is of good or poor quality.

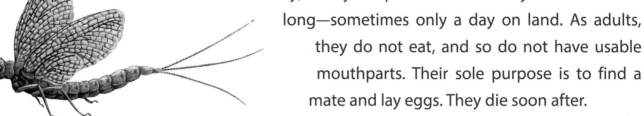

Some mayflies are most active at dawn and dusk, making them crepuscular. Unfortunately, nearly all species of adult mayflies do not live long—sometimes only a day on land. As adults, they do not eat, and so do not have usable mouthparts. Their sole purpose is to find a mate and lay eggs. They die soon after.

---

# Lightning Bugs

Different insects have adaptations for communicating, such as chirping, singing, or, in the case of lightning bugs, lighting up. This is called bioluminescence. Male lightning bugs flash to attract a mate. The females flash to respond. Different species of lightning bugs flash different patterns.

Lightning bugs, also called fireflies, are a type of beetle. They produce a chemical called luciferase, which is an enzyme that, when combined with another compound called luciferin, creates light. Scientists study lightning bugs and luciferase to learn more about the health of humans. Luciferase is now used to detect blood clots, as well as to detect a chemical that may be linked to cancer and diabetes.

## Author's Note

As a child, I was both grossed out by and petrified of insects and other creepy crawlies. I remember spotting a centipede on my wall in the middle of the night and being so scared of it, I couldn't even go downstairs to tell my parents.

It wasn't until my first year of teaching that things changed. Someone showed me a copy of the current *National Geographic* (March 1998) that featured a twenty-page article on beetles, and I was blown away. I had never thought of insects as small machines with incredible adaptations as well as works of art, but the article and photographs opened my eyes to the world of insects, as well as science.

I went out and bought my own copy of the magazine, and my life changed forever. I ended up going back to school to get my Master of Education in Science Education. I left teaching for a while to work at a nature museum, where I wrote science lessons and got training in various insects, such as cockroaches! And then I also started writing, mostly about science topics (thirty-seven books and articles), including another book on insects. My life had completely changed, all because of the mesmerizing photographs of a creature that once caused me to freeze in terror.

I hope that you can learn to appreciate insects, spiders, and even centipedes. And, once you understand them, I hope you can see their beauty and be as awestruck by them as I am.